Velociraptor
Up Close

Swift Dinosaur

Zoom
In on
Dinosaurs!

Peter Dodson, PhD

Illustrated by Bob Walters and Laura Fields

CONTENTS

WORDS TO KNOW

dinosaurs (DY noh sorz)—Reptiles that lived from about 230 million years ago to 65 million years ago. They had a special kind of hip and long legs.

fossils (FAH sulz)—Parts of living things from long ago. They often turn to stone.

mammal (MA muhl)—An animal that can grow fur and make milk for its young.

predator (PREH duh tur)—An animal that hunts other animals for food.

prey (PRAY)—An animal that a predator eats.

raptor (RAP tur)—A kind of bird that hunts and has sharp claws on its feet. *Raptor* is also the name of a group of small, meat-eating dinosaurs.

Pronunciation Guide

Deinonychus [dy NAH nih kus]

Dromaeosaurus [droh MAY oh SAWR us]

Microraptor [MY kroh RAP tur]

Oviraptor [OH vih RAP tur]

Protoceratops [PROH toh SAIR uh tops]

Utahraptor [YOO tah RAP tur]

Velociraptor [vuh LAH sih RAP tur]

A Speedy Thief

Velociraptor was a little, fast-running **dinosaur**.

It had sharp teeth and pointy claws.

It was a **predator**.

It chased other animals to eat.

Dinosaurs did not have to be huge to be fierce!

Body

Velociraptor was about 6 feet long.
That's about the size of a man.

It was 20 inches tall at the hips.
It weighed 30 pounds.
That's about the same as a large turkey.

Velociraptor probably had bumpy scales
on its body, just like all dinosaurs.

Scales and Feathers

Over millions of years, some kinds of dinosaurs changed a little at a time. They became more and more like birds.

In 2007, scientists learned something new! *Velociraptor* had feathers on its arms. It may have had fuzzy feathers on other parts of its body, too.

Velociraptor's arm bones had bumps on them. This show where the feathers once attached.

Tail

Velociraptor had a long, stiff tail.

The tail helped *Velociraptor* to balance or turn.

This means it was an active animal!

Claws
and Feet

Velociraptor walked on two legs.

Each foot had three toes.

The inside toe on each foot was held up off the ground. It had a large, curved claw.

Velociraptor could kick and slash at its **prey** with this sharp claw.

It could also use the claw to climb trees.

Hunting for Food

Velociraptor had 60 small, sharp teeth.

It ate whatever it could catch.
It ate insects, lizards, and other
small animals.

Sometimes it attacked large prey.

Its dinner might have weighed more
than it did!

Babies

Velociraptor was very tiny when it hatched.

We do not know how many eggs were laid in its nest.

The babies grew slowly.

Velociraptor lived about 15 years.

Home

Velociraptor lived in a dry, sandy area.

The wind blew sand into hills.

Sometimes the hills buried animals. The animals became **fossils**.

One special fossil shows *Velociraptor* attacking *Protoceratops*. During their fight, they were covered in sand.

Over time, they turned into fossils.

A *Protoceratops* and *Velociraptor* turned into a fossil. They were fighting when they died.

Velociraptor Was Not Alone

Oviraptor

Protoceratops

Protoceratops and *Oviraptor* lived with *Velociraptor*.

Protoceratops was a small, horned dinosaur.

Oviraptor was a meat eater that had no teeth. Maybe it ate eggs or insects.

Turtles and small crocodiles lived in the water.

Small furry **mammals**, lizards, and insects lived on the land.

Where on Earth?

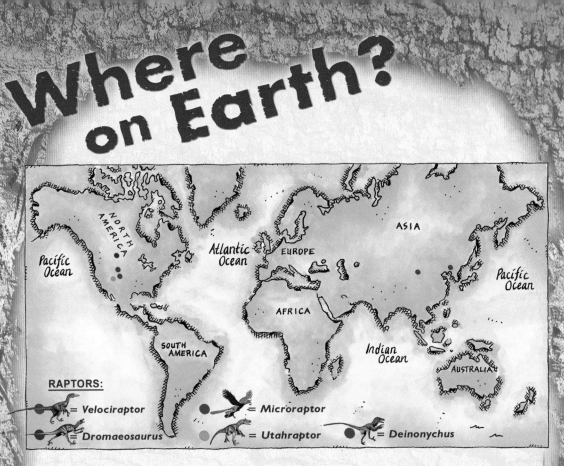

Velociraptor lived 70 to 80 million years ago. About ten fossil skeletons have been found. They show scientists that these dinosaurs lived in Mongolia and China. Mongolia is a country next to China.

Just as you may have cousins and other relatives, *Velociraptor* had relatives, too! Scientists know this because they were all **raptors** with a large, curved claw on their inner toes.

Microraptor lived in China. *Utahraptor* lived in Utah. *Dromaeosaurus* lived in Canada. *Deinonychus* lived in Montana and Wyoming.

Learn More

Books

Burnie, David. *First Dinosaur Picture Atlas.* New York: Kingfisher, 2008.

Lindeen, Carol K. *Velociraptors.* Mankato, Minn.: Capstone Press, 2006.

Nunn, Daniel. *Velociraptor.* Chicago: Heinemann Library, 2007.

Web Sites

Dino Database: *Velociraptor.* <http://www.kidsdinos.com/dinosaurs-for-children.php?dinosaur=Velociraptor>

Dinosaur World: *Velociraptor mongoliensis.* <http://www.dinosaur-world.com/feathered_dinosaurs/velociraptor_mongoliensis.htm>

Enchanted Learning: *Velociraptor Fact Sheet.* <http://www.enchantedlearning.com/subjects/dinosaurs/facts/Velociraptor/>

INDEX

For Jonah Emile

Bailey Books, an imprint of Enslow Publishers, Inc.

Copyright © 2011 by Peter Dodson

All rights reserved.

No part of this book may be reproduced by any means without the written permission of the publisher.

Library of Congress Cataloging-in-Publication Data

Dodson, Peter.

Velociraptor up close : swift dinosaur / by Peter Dodson.

p. cm. — (Zoom in on dinosaurs!)

Summary: "Gives young readers an up-close look at Velociraptor and how its features helped it live"—Provided by publisher.

Includes bibliographical references and index.

ISBN 978-0-7660-3337-5

1. Velociraptor—Juvenile literature. I. Title.

QE862.S3D6385 2011

567.912—dc22   2009021276

Printed in the United States of America

062010 Lake Book Manufacturing, Inc., Melrose Park, IL

10 9 8 7 6 5 4 3 2 1

Illustration Credits: Bob Walters and Laura Fields

Cover Illustration: Bob Walters and Laura Fields

To Our Readers: We have done our best to make sure all Interne Addresses in this book were active and appropriate when we went to press However, the author and the publisher have no control over and assum no liability for the material available on those Internet sites or on other We sites they may link to. Any comments or suggestions can be sent by e-ma to comments@enslow.com or to the address on the back cover.

Enslow Publishers, Inc., is committed to printing our books on recycle paper. The paper in every book contains 10% to 30% post-consumer wast (PCW). The cover board on the outside of each book contains 100% PCW Our goal is to do our part to help young people and the environment too!

Note to Parents and Teachers: The *Zoom In on Dinosaurs!* series supports th National Science Education Standards for K–4 science. The Words to Kno section introduces subject-specific vocabulary words, including pronunciatio and definitions. Early readers may need help with these new words.

Allan A. De Fina, PhD
Series Literacy Consultant
Dean, College of Education
Professor of Literacy Education
New Jersey City University
Past President of the New Jersey Reading Association

Philip J. Currie, PhD
Series Science Consultant
Professor of Dinosaur Paleobiolo
University of Alberta
Edmonton, Alberta
Canada

Bailey Books
an imprint of
Enslow Publishers, Inc.
40 Industrial Road
Box 398
Berkeley Heights, NJ 07922
USA
http://www.enslow.com